WORLD ORGANIZATIONS

UNICEF

Katherine Prior

W
FRANKLIN WATTS
LONDON • SYDNEY

This edition 2004
Franklin Watts
96 Leonard Street, London EC2A 4XD

Franklin Watts Australia
45–51 Huntley Street
Alexandria NSW 2015

Series editor: Rachel Cooke
Editor: Sarah Ridley
Designer: Simon Borrough
Picture research: Sue Mennell

This book has been checked by UNICEF for factual
accuracy, but this is not a UNICEF publication and
does not necessarily reflect the views or policy of
UNICEF.

A CIP catalogue record for this book is available
from the British Library.

ISBN   0 7496 5696 4
Dewey classification 362.7

Printed in Malaysia

Picture credits:
Cover pictures: Panos Pictures: tr (Jeremy
Hartley); Still Pictures: 1 (Ron Giling);
UNICEF: br
Insides: Panos Pictures pp. 2t (Liba Taylor), 5t
(Trygve Bolstad), 6 (Crispin Hughes), 7l
(Martin Adler), 7r (Jeremy Hartley), 15t (Tim
Hetherington), 17 (Liba Taylor), 22l (Liba
Taylor), 22r (Crispin Hughes), 23l (Howard
Davies), 23r (Howard Davies), 25 (Lana
Wong), 26t (Giacomo Pirozzi)
Still Pictures pp. 1l (Mark Edwards), 1r (Ron
Giling), 4l (Ron Giling), 5b (Ron Giling), 8
(Ron Giling), 12b (Ron Giling), 13t (Hartmut
Schwarzbach), 16 (Mark Edwards), 18
(Shehzad Noorani), 19t (Shehzad Noorani),
20b (Shehzad Noorani), 21 (Reinhard Janke), 24
(Jorgen Schytte), 26b (Ron Giling), 28t (John
Maier), 29t (David Hoffman)
UNICEF pp. 2-3 (HQ99-0440/Radhika Chalasani),
3, 4r, 9t (ICEF-0318), 9b (HQ98-0787/Jeremy
Horner), 10 (ICEF-0355), 11(ICEF-2371), 12t (HQ93-
1893), 13b (HQ00-0440/Radhika Chalasani), 14
(HQ470-0001), 15b (HQ00-0283/Giacomo Pirozzi), 19b
(HQ93-0113/Roger Lemoyne), 20t (HQ00-0250/Giacomo
Pirozzi), 27 (HQ99-0623/Giacomo Pirozzi), 28b (HQ91-
0137/Patricio Baeza), 29b (C76 19/Ruby Mera)

Contents

unicef
United Nations Children's Fund

The United Nations Children's Fund (UNICEF for short) is an organization devoted to improving the lives of children all round the world. UNICEF is part of the United Nations, which tries to maintain peace worldwide. The main purpose of UNICEF is to make sure that children everywhere get the care and education they need to grow into happy, healthy adults.

Children are special

UNICEF believes that children are a unique group of people who have human rights that *must* be protected, such as the right to education, to a caring family or to good healthcare. Children are not small adults, who simply need less of what adults need. Children's minds and bodies require special types of care and affection; if they do not get these when they are young, their lives can be harmed for ever.

 Spotlight

The UNICEF emblem shows that it is part of the United Nations. The United Nations' own emblem is a globe of the world, supported by two olive branches. An olive branch is a symbol of peace, so together the globe and olive branch symbolize world peace. UNICEF uses this emblem, but inside the globe it adds a picture of an adult holding a baby.

United Nations Children's Fund

▲ *The UNICEF emblem shows that it cares about the welfare of children and their parents all over the world.*

▶ *Education is a basic human right. Every child, like this Bangladeshi girl, has the right to go to school.*

UNICEF encourages governments everywhere to value their country's children and to put their rights first. If there is no hope for a country's children, there can be no hope for a country's future.

▶ *A young boy does an adult's work in a brick factory in Bangladesh.*

▼ *A Ghanaian boy cheerfully campaigns against child labour.*

Spotlight

In 2004, UNICEF celebrated ten years of its global 'Change for Good' campaign, to improve the lives of poor children. Mexico City, where thousands of children live and work on the streets, is one of many places to have benefited from the campaign. Here, UNICEF works to improve access to education for street children, and to combat the violence and abuse they face.

WORK IS ONLY FOR ADULTS

Children are equal

UNICEF treats all children equally. It does not make a distinction between different religions, races or nationalities, or between boys and girls. UNICEF believes that all children should be able to look forward to a full and active life.

▼ *Children have the right to a fair standard of living. This Angolan mother struggles to look after her baby in a bombed-out flat.*

 Checklist

The Convention on the Rights of the Child describes the human rights that every child in the world is born with. The Convention is a treaty which most nations have ratified. It was formally accepted by the General Assembly of the United Nations in 1989. The Convention includes the children's rights:

- to healthcare
- to education
- to a fair standard of living
- to leisure and play
- to protection from exploitation and abuse

 Spotlight

"I became a soldier to avenge the death of my father," says Martin, aged 13, who was a child-soldier in Sierra Leone. "I came home one day to find him dead and my school burnt down."

Martin was one of about 6,000 children used as soldiers in the civil war in the west African country of Sierra Leone. There are many child-soldiers like Martin in countries such as Angola, Liberia and Sierra Leone. UNICEF campaigns for help for these children and for an end to the

Child survival

UNICEF supports projects which help children in over 150 countries. Many of these projects aim to keep children alive and healthy. Malnutrition, a lack of good food, harms children in particular. Many illnesses caused by malnutrition can be cured or prevented with better foods and vitamins. Common childhood diseases, like polio and measles, can be prevented with vaccines. Diseases carried by water and dirt can be prevented by providing clean drinking water and toilet facilities.

UNICEF works with governments and community groups to cure these problems. It has a duty to spend its money on helping those children who need it most. This means that much work is directed at developing countries, such as the poorer countries of Africa, Asia and Latin America. UNICEF uses child mortality rates to tell which countries need urgent assistance in improving health care for their children.

 Spotlight

In the African country of Angola 292 children out of every 1,000 born each year, will die before the age of five. This high child mortality rate is a tragedy for Angola – both for the children whose lives are wasted, and for their parents who have to watch them die.

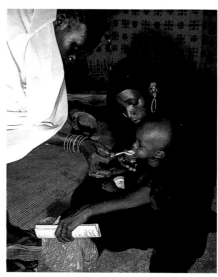

▲ In Sudan, a country which has suffered a lot from war and famine, a sick child is given emergency food aid.

◀ UNICEF helps refugees, such as these people in the Democratic Republic of Congo, who have been forced to flee their homes through war.

▲ *A mother attends a school for adults in Senegal. Education gives her and her baby a better chance in life.*

Children's welfare

Children don't just need good health. UNICEF works over the long term to break the cycle of poverty that often leaves children and their mothers suffering the most. Children often miss out on school, as their parents did before them, because they need to work to help their families survive. UNICEF supports projects to help their parents earn a better living.

UNICEF helps parents to be better carers and encourages governments to put children first when they make new laws and decisions. Poverty, homelessness and poor school attendance can occur in any country, so UNICEF works for children's rights to be respected everywhere, but it only runs programmes in poor countries.

 Checklist

In preparation for the Special Session of the United Nations General Assembly on Children in 2002, the 'Say Yes for Children' campaign gained the support of nearly 100 million people around the world. These supporters called for action on ten steps to improve children's lives:

1. Educate every child
2. Leave no child out
3. Fight poverty: invest in children
4. Care for every child
5. Stop harming and exploiting children
6. Fight HIV/AIDS
7. Listen to children
8. Put children first
9. Protect the Earth for children
10. Protect children from war

UNICEF first started work in 1946 in Europe. The Second World War had just ended and many towns and villages had been wrecked by bombing and fires. Farms were not growing much food, factories had stopped working and shops had nothing to sell. Children suffered most in this chaos.

▼ *In Greece, after World War II, a small boy clutches a blanket that has been given to him by UNICEF workers.*

The United Nations and UNICEF

The United Nations had been set up after the war to try to keep the peace. Countries who joined the United Nations sent delegates who worked to find peaceful ways of fixing the world's problems. These delegates questioned whether Europe could recover from the war if it did not do something about its children.

In 1946, the delegates decided to create a fund to help the children of post-war Europe. This was called the United Nations International Children's Emergency Fund – UNICEF for short. The fund would help children of all nationalities – not just the children in countries that had won the war.

● Spotlight

In 1948, the Red Cross in Scandinavia asked UNICEF to help it fight tuberculosis (TB), a deadly disease of the lungs that can be prevented by giving people a vaccine.

UNICEF supplied the Red Cross with enough vaccine and sterile needles to vaccinate hundreds of thousands of children against TB. Since these early days, UNICEF has organized thousands of mass immunization campaigns.

▲ *UNICEF's international supply centre is in the Danish city of Copenhagen. The centre provides medicines, books and other supplies for health and education campaigns all over the world.*

Life-giving milk

UNICEF's first leaders believed that their immediate job was to improve children's health and diet. One way to do this was to supply milk to children and babies. The war had destroyed many dairies in Europe so milk was scarce and expensive. UNICEF worked with local leaders, charities and farmers to improve their milk production. UNICEF wanted to be sure that when it left a town or district, the local people knew how to keep the milk production flowing.

In all its projects, UNICEF works with the people it is trying to help to find a lasting way of improving their children's lives. UNICEF provides the money, training and technology and then local people run the project themselves.

▲ *After World War II, many European children had poor diets. Here, in 1951, Greek school children drink milk provided by UNICEF workers.*

UNICEF goes worldwide

When UNICEF was created in 1946, it was meant to be a temporary organization. By about 1950, the United Nations was ready to close down UNICEF because conditions for children in Europe had improved. Pakistan's delegate to the United Nations protested. How, he asked, could the United Nations say that UNICEF had finished its work, when children were dying all over the world?

The other delegates agreed. In 1953, UNICEF was made a permanent part of the United Nations with a duty to improve the health and welfare of all the world's children. It was at this time that its full name was shortened to the United Nations Children's Fund.

Problem

UNICEF was created to deal with the emergency caused by the Second World War. It is still one of UNICEF's main aims to respond rapidly to the suffering caused by war and natural disaster.

Soon, however, child health workers began to talk about a 'silent emergency' affecting millions of the world's children. This 'silent emergency' was caused by the problems of poverty and disease that, over time, killed or hurt many more children than war. Today, it is on these 'silent emergencies' in the poor countries of the world that UNICEF spends most money.

◀ UNICEF helps countries fight preventable diseases. In the 1950s, UNICEF helped Indonesia vaccinate millions of its children against the disease tuberculosis (TB).

UNICEF is not an ordinary charity, as it is part of the United Nations. It is the only United Nations organization devoted exclusively to children and women.

The Executive Director and the Executive Board

UNICEF's head is the Executive Director, who is appointed by the General Assembly of the United Nations. It is the Executive Director's job to tell world leaders and other powerful people about UNICEF's work and persuade them to assist it. UNICEF's present Executive Director is an American woman, Carol Bellamy, who was first appointed in 1995.

UNICEF's central organization is the Executive Board. It has 36 members, all chosen from countries that belong to the United Nations. The Executive Board holds regular meetings at UNICEF's headquarters in New York. It decides which projects UNICEF should undertake and ensures that there is the money to pay for them. The Board also examines the success of past projects, and identifies mistakes that should be avoided in the future.

◀ Carol Bellamy, UNICEF's Executive Director

▼ Part of the United Nations, UNICEF has its headquarters in New York.

The regional offices and country offices

Besides its New York headquarters, UNICEF has 7 regional offices and 126 country offices. The regional offices organize all of UNICEF's work in a particular region, such as Latin America or Eastern Europe. The country offices are the real centres of the work. They co-ordinate the health, sanitation and education projects in each country where UNICEF works.

▼ UNICEF helps people learn about the dangers of landmines – deadly bombs left in the soil after a war.

▶ At a refugee camp in Albania, children play games that help them recover from the horrible things they have seen in war. UNICEF funds many programmes like this one.

Who pays for UNICEF?

In 2002 UNICEF spent US$1,454 million (approximately £760 million). Over half of this money was given voluntarily by governments. Often a government gives money for a particular project. In June 2000, for example, the Japanese government gave US$28.6 million (nearly £18 million) to UNICEF for its campaign against polio.

UNICEF also gets money from private companies, charities and the general public. Ever since it first began, UNICEF has appealed directly to members of the public for donations. The organization's 37 National Committees persuade people in wealthier countries to donate money to help children in poorer parts of the world.

▼ *The first UNICEF card, drawn by Jitka Samkova.*

Spotlight

In 1947, Jitka Samkova, a 7-year-old Czech girl, painted a picture to say thank you to UNICEF for helping her village after the Second World War. UNICEF printed Jitka's picture on greeting cards and sold them to raise money. Since then UNICEF has sold over four thousand million greeting cards, raising US$1,000 million. Many famous artists let UNICEF use their pictures for free to illustrate the cards.

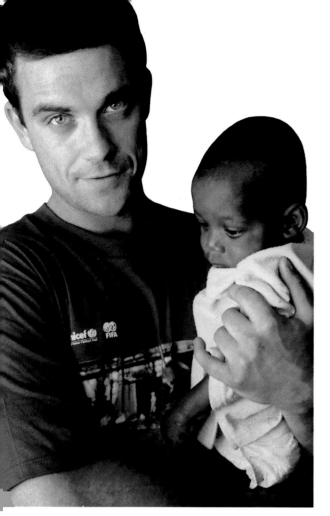

UNICEF enlists famous people to help it raise money. These celebrities are called Goodwill Ambassadors. They visit UNICEF projects and help publicize the organization's work, as well as showing donors how their money is being spent and encouraging them to give more. In 2003, the Colombian pop star Shakira, aged 26, became the youngest Goodwill Ambassador – UNICEF hoped she would publicize its work to a younger audience.

How is UNICEF's money spent?

UNICEF spends most of its money on equipment, supplies and 'logistics'. Logistics means the activities that make a project work. Providing transportation for health workers and storage for medicines is part of logistics. Printing and handing out posters to tell people about an Immunization Day is also part of logistics.

▲ *In May 2000, pop-star Robbie Williams visited Mozambique to meet children whose parents have been killed by the disease AIDS. Many live in homes or attend play centres that are funded by UNICEF.*

UNICEF tries to keep staff costs down. It employs fewer than 6,000 people in posts in over 150 countries. Almost 5,000 of these employees work in UNICEF's country offices. The UNICEF staff work with the people who can change children's lives, such as government ministers for health and education, or they work training local people how to help children. UNICEF wants the people who make donations to know that their money really does reach children in need.

◀ *Nelson Mandela and Graça Machel are two political figures using their voice and influence to improve children's lives.*

Many childhood illnesses are caused by the problems that come with poverty: malnutrition, dirty water and lack of skills and education. UNICEF tries to prevent these illnesses, but sadly, there is no magical drug which cures poverty.

Clean water for health

Clean water is a basic need for human beings. Many children suffer from illnesses such as diarrhoea, cholera and typhoid because their drinking water is polluted and their toilet facilities are dirty. To many people, particularly those in poor villages, it would seem like a miracle to switch on a tap and get clean water.

Since 1970, UNICEF has run many projects to change this, helping governments and communities to improve water supplies and sanitation in rural areas in countries such as Bangladesh, India, Nigeria and Sudan. In these projects, UNICEF uses simple technology, such as drilling new wells in the ground and fitting them with sturdy hand-pumps. UNICEF also teaches people about good hygiene and how to look after their water supplies.

◀ *Hand-pumps, like this one in Burkina Faso, provide clean water.*

▲ *Water that people walk in is dangerous to drink. UNICEF helps provide clean water supplies for villagers.*

 ## Spotlight

In 2000, UNICEF supported a new project that has given hundreds of families living in the poorer areas of Harare in Zimbabwe access to clean, low-cost toilets, in or near their homes. As always, UNICEF worked with the local people in the design and planning of this project so that maintenance of the toilets will

 ## Problem

Often the medical answer to a child's illness seems simple. For example, if a baby who has diarrhoea is fed with a mixture of salt and sugar dissolved in clean water it will survive. This mixture is called an oral rehydration solution and is a very cheap way of saving a baby's life.

Given this, why do babies still die from diarrhoea? In poor countries, many mothers cannot read, so they cannot understand the instructions printed on packets of oral rehydration mix. Many poor families do not have clean water in which to mix the solution. Some do not know that if they boil water for ten minutes, it will become safe to drink. Or they cannot afford the fuel to boil the water for that amount of time.

All of these extra problems explain why diarrhoea kills

Helping mothers help their children

Parents are the most important people in a child's life, particularly the mother. She is usually the one who decides what to feed her child and nurses her child through illnesses. The mother is often the only teacher a child has before attending school.

In wealthier countries, governments run pregnancy classes and mother-and-baby centres. These give information and support to women from the time when they become pregnant up until their child is ready to start school. Many mothers around the world do not have access to this sort of help and advice. Many women die from problems with their pregnancy or while they are giving birth. Many others do not know how to help their baby when illness strikes.

 At a health centre in Sudan, a UNICEF worker shows a pregnant woman what vitamins and minerals she needs to take to give birth to a healthy baby.

Spotlight

UNICEF helps pregnant women in 57 countries to obtain folic acid tablets to help their unborn children. Folic acid is a vitamin needed to make our blood work properly.

UNICEF helps these mothers. It trains local health workers to advise mothers about diet, hygiene and preventable illnesses. Projects focus on teaching mothers to read so they can get information for themselves from health posters and pamphlets, baby books and the instructions on medicines. Improving mothers' education is one of the best ways of improving children's health.

Educating mothers can also help them secure a better future for themselves and their children. UNICEF is helping many projects that encourage mothers to contribute to their families' economic well-being with an income of their own.

▶ *Community workers in Bangladesh use pictures and posters to give rural women basic health advice.*

 ## Spotlight

In 1991, UNICEF and other agencies began a scheme to make hospitals 'baby-friendly'. Baby-friendly hospitals help mothers give their babies the best start in life. They encourage mothers to breast-feed their babies, as breast-milk helps the baby's resistance to disease and is also much cheaper than artificial milk. Baby-friendly hospitals let mothers keep their babies with them, rather than in a separate room. Mexico was the first country to encourage all its hospitals to become baby-friendly. UNICEF is working with the UK health service to make hospitals more baby-friendly in the UK.

▲ *A Chinese baby gets breast-fed on the move!*

Making children stronger with Vitamin A

Vitamin A is a nutrient that everybody needs. It is found in fish, milk, eggs, carrots and leafy greens, such as spinach. People who do not eat enough of these foods are prone to eye infections and can become blind. Children who lack Vitamin A are more likely to die if they get sick.

Many children who live in poverty lack Vitamin A. The problem can be cured, however, by giving children two small and cheap Vitamin A doses a year. UNICEF supports a worldwide programme to distribute tablets and capsules to countries where Vitamin A shortage is a problem. UNICEF knows that taking extra Vitamin A does not fix the problem of poverty, but it hopes to keep children alive while their governments find ways to improve the general standard of living.

▼ UNICEF helps grow vegetables in an aid project in Sudan.

▶ A toddler in Mozambique receives Vitamin A.

and illnesses

Young children get sick more often than adults do. In Europe and North America, most babies are immunized (given vaccines) against the serious childhood diseases, such as measles, diphtheria, polio, TB and tetanus. Unfortunately, in poor countries, many children are not immunized and they are regularly harmed, or even killed, by these diseases.

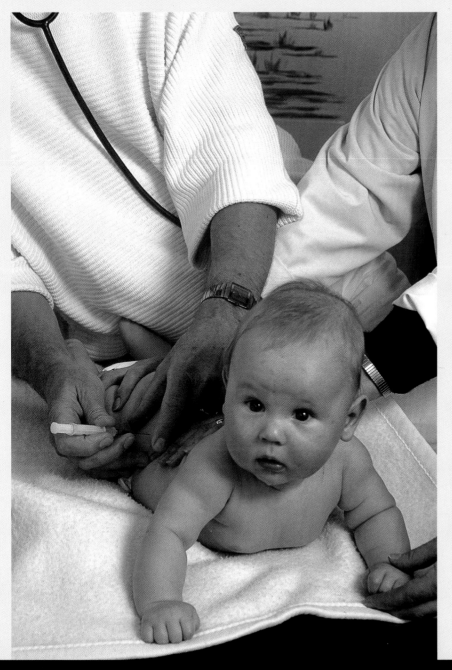

Vaccines and immunization

Vaccines work by teaching the body's immune system how to recognize what a disease looks like and making it grow special proteins that will attack the germs or viruses that cause that disease. Some vaccines are given by injection. Others can be swallowed like cough medicine. Some vaccines need to be given more than once to be really effective.

◀ For children in wealthy countries, like this baby from Germany, it is normal to be immunized against common childhood diseases.

Unfortunately, in poorer countries there are often not enough vaccines or health centres to care for all the population. Sometimes parents have never heard of immunization – they do not know how it can help their children. Every year, nearly two million children die from diseases that could have been prevented with vaccines. UNICEF works to stop these unnecessary deaths.

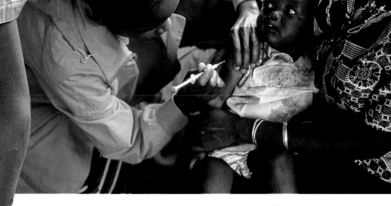

◀ *Polio has crippled this Zimbabwean boy for life.*

▲ *A Kenyan baby is immunized against tetanus.*

Days of Tranquillity

When a country is at war, the fighting often makes it impossible for parents to get their children immunized. To help such children UNICEF helps organize Days of Tranquillity, or peace. These are days when enemy soldiers agree to stop fighting each other to allow medical teams to immunize local children. It takes time and patience to persuade enemies to lay down their guns for a day, but the rewards for children's health are worth it.

Spotlight

Massive efforts by UNICEF and its partners – including the World Health Organization and Rotary International – mean that polio may be totally eradicated by 2008. This is because of major immunization campaigns, such as that in 2002, when more than 500 million children received vaccinations in 93 countries. It is important, however, that children are vaccinated several times to be immune for life.

▶ *This poster in Nepal tells parents about a Polio Immunization Day.*

▼ *Children in Tanzania are immunized against measles.*

National Immunization Days

UNICEF helps poor countries fight preventable diseases by supporting National Immunization Days. These are days when a country immunizes as many of its young people as possible. UNICEF's workers do not do everything themselves. Instead they work with the country's health department, medical staff, schools, charities, and community leaders. Together, they make sure that there is enough vaccine available for the day's work and enough trained volunteers to administer it.

सानो थोपा ठूलो सुरक्षा

५ वर्ष सम्मका सबै बाल-बालिकाहरुलाई
पोलियो थोपा खुवाऔं
पोलियो रोगबाट बचाऔं

मसिर २२ गते (आइतबार) र २०५४ माघ ५ गते (आइतबा

प्य सेवा विभाग

सहयोगी संस्थाहरू
• UK / DFID • Govt. of Japan • Rotary International

Many of the world's oldest diseases can now be prevented or cured, but what happens when a new disease appears? Since the 1980s the disease AIDS has killed millions of people. Scientists are trying to find a cure for AIDS or a vaccine against it, but meanwhile people continue to die.

In Africa AIDS is an emergency. There, more than 12 million children under the age of 15 have seen their parents die from the disease. In Uganda alone, AIDS has made one child out of every ten an orphan. Often left to look after themselves, these children struggle to survive. AIDS is destroying their future and if AIDS is not stopped soon, it will set back the progress that UNICEF has helped to make in improving general health in Africa.

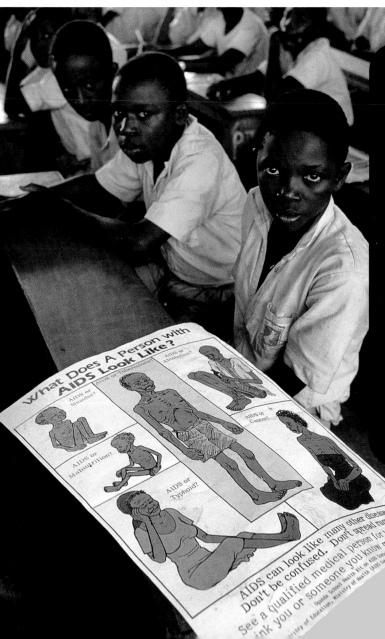

✔ Checklist

Numbers of children in African countries whose mother or both parents have died of AIDS:

- Nigeria   1,000,000
- Ethiopia   990,000
- Kenya   890,000
- Uganda   880,000
- Tanzania   810,000
- Zimbabwe   780,000
- Zambia   570,000

UNICEF is helping to run many projects for these children but a cure to the disease is the real answer.

◀ *School children in Uganda are taught about the disease AIDS, which is killing millions of people in Uganda and other African countries.*

Babies need iodine

Some illnesses are caused by what people eat. Iodine is a chemical that everybody needs to be healthy. It exists naturally in soil so most people get all the iodine they need from root vegetables, such as potatoes and onions. In some very wet or hilly areas, however, the soil's iodine has been washed away by rain.

Pregnant women who lack iodine are likely to give birth to babies who are mentally disabled. Similarly young children's brains can be damaged by a lack of iodine in their diet. Sometimes they become unable to learn even simple things.

One solution is to add iodine to salt – a food that everybody eats. This is called iodized salt. Since the 1980s, UNICEF has helped governments and private companies make and market iodized salt all over the world. Iodized salt saves around 12 million babies a year from the danger of mental disability.

Spotlight

In June 2003 the Vlora Salt Factory in Albania began producing iodized salt for the first time in the country's history. UNICEF worked with the government to introduce the change and provided equipment to the factory. The production of iodized salt is vital: before 2003, 60 per cent of Albanian children lacked enough iodine in their diet.

▼ This Kenyan family suffers from not having enough iodine in their diet. This has made their child very weak.

UNICEF helps children receive the very best care from birth, when a good start to life can make a big difference in their health and well-being. During the school years, UNICEF helps children learn in good schools that have a friendly environment. And in adolescence, UNICEF helps ensure children get the loving support they need from families, schools and communities. UNICEF believes that you can best help children by listening to them and encouraging them to participate in various ways at home and in the community.

The importance of education

UNICEF supports projects that educate parents on how to teach their very young children through play, and it campaigns against child labour that denies so many school-age children an education. By supporting programmes that strive for a good education to keep children interested in learning, UNICEF hopes that many more children will rise out of poverty in the future.

▲ *UNICEF funds games and schooling for these children made homeless by the war in Sierra Leone.*

▶ *Liberian children play football. Every child has the right to play.*

⬤ Spotlight

Amela lives in the former Yugoslav Republic of Macedonia. She is just one of the four-year-olds who have benefited from the Lifestart Programme which is partly funded by UNICEF. Each month a health worker visits her home to talk with her mother about good parenting. He also gives Amela a poem or song to learn and lends her a new toy to play with over the next month. As there are few playgroups in her country, this early stimulation for Amela is vital.

▲ *UNICEF helped repair this primary school in Iraq, after it had been damaged in the first Gulf War in 1991. War can badly interrupt children's schooling.*

✓ Checklist

Some of UNICEF's recent projects in education:
• in 2003, more than 1 million people took part in the world's largest simultaneous lesson, to highlight the importance of education for girls
• in 2002, UNICEF helped 3 million children return to school in war-torn Afghanistan
• in 1999, UNICEF helped 96,000 children receive primary schooling in the refugee camps of Tanzania
• in Brazil, a programme provided education to 50,000 children who work in garbage dumps collecting waste to sell
• in Nicaragua, 175,000 extremely poor children, or children who work, were given the opportunity to go to schools that offered classes at times to suit the children's needs.

Looking out for girls

UNICEF tries especially hard to get girls to attend school. In many countries, in particular in South Asia and the Middle East, daughters are often not as valued as sons. Girls are kept at home to do the housework and look after the smaller children. Girls miss out in other ways too as they are often not as well fed as their brothers. If they fall sick, their families often do not spend as much money on medicines for them.

UNICEF believes that all children deserve the same start in life, girls as well as boys. It also knows that many girls will become mothers one day. If girls are not healthy and educated, they will be less likely to care well for their own children.

Problems in cities

In the fast-growing cities of Latin America, such as São Paulo in Brazil, the number of homeless children has become an emergency. Hundreds of thousands of children, some as young as six, are trying to earn their own living on city streets. They have no proper home or education. These children are often regarded as criminals and are rounded up by the police and thrown into jail.

Since 1981, UNICEF has worked with charities in Latin America and elsewhere to help children like these. It funds a range of projects: reading classes, soup kitchens, health check-ups, advice centres and sports. It also works with governments to help these children fulfill their rights to good healthcare, education and protection.

▲ Homeless children sleep on the pavement outside a TV shop in Brazil.
▼ At a UNICEF-funded home for Bolivian children who live or work on the streets, boys learn about electricity.

 Spotlight

Kalpana dreams of being a cook when she grows up. She also wants to get married and have a nice house. Kalpana lives on the platforms at Sealdah railway station in Calcutta, India. Calcutta has thousands of homeless children like Kalpana. She is one of the lucky ones because a local charity, called Cini-Asha, gives school lessons and other support to these railway children. UNICEF helps by giving money to charities like Cini-Asha so that they can continue their work.

There are forgotten children in the wealthy cities of the world also. Since the mid-1990s UNICEF has been drawing attention to these children who often live in poverty and miss school. That they live this way in societies where so many live in comfort is all the more shocking.

▲ Teenagers sleep in a shop doorway in London. Homelessness affects children in rich countries too.

Spotlight

As part of its aim to educate people about children's rights, UNICEF has helped create clever cartoons that are shown worldwide. Using pictures and sounds only, they can be understood by people in any country.

Spotlight

Zahid comes from a village in Pakistan. Even though he is only seven, he already works like an adult, stitching footballs all day. "I don't play with the footballs I make," says Zahid, "I just work. But I'd love to watch a match on television."

UNICEF is working with governments and big sports companies to stop the use of footballs that have been made by children and to give more poor children opportunities to go to school. Slowly, the number of children making footballs in Pakistan is falling.

Working for the future

In 2002, more than 7,000 people took part in the Special Session of the United Nations General Assembly on Children. The Session reviewed progress since the 1990 World Summit for Children, which set goals for children's well-being. At the same time, the Session looked at what new steps it could take to improve children's rights. Carol Bellamy, UNICEF's Executive Director, ensured that hundreds of children took part in the Session. They met with world leaders and discussed issues affecting their lives.

◀ The 1990 World Summit for Children, New York.

Glossary

child mortality rate the number of children, out of every thousand born, who die before their fifth birthday

convention an agreement or contract signed by different countries on an important issue

dehydration the loss of body fluids through an illness such as diarrhoea

diarrhoea a disorder or sickness of the intestines which gives a person a very upset stomach and causes loss of water from his or her body

executive a person concerned with making decisions and policies; UNICEF's Executive Board decides what projects the organization should support

exploitation taking unfair advantage of people who cannot protect themselves

hygiene the science of maintaining good health

malnutrition poor health and slow growth caused by a bad diet

mortality death

nutrient something that provides nourishment; a food or chemical that everyone needs for good health

oral by mouth; an oral vaccine is one that is swallowed

preventable disease a disease that can be easily stopped, perhaps by a vaccine, or a better diet or a clean water supply

rehydration replacing fluid lost through diarrhoea or vomiting

sanitation keeping people healthy by providing clean living conditions, such as clean water and hygienic toilets

vaccine a medicine which stops someone from getting a particular disease; some vaccines are swallowed; others are given as injections

vitamins natural chemical substances present in foods which, in very small doses, are essential for good health

New York Headquarters of UNICEF:
UNICEF House
3 United Nations Plaza
New York, New York 10017
U.S.A.
www.unicef.org

UNICEF Innocenti Research Centre:
Spedale Degli Innocenti
Piazza SS. Annunziata, 12
50122 Florence
Italy
www.unicef-icdc.org

Some UNICEF National Committees:
Each UNICEF Committee supports a variety of different projects so it is worth visiting more than one website.

UNICEF Committee of Australia
P.O. Box A 2005
Sydney South
NSW 1235
Australia
www.unicef.com.au

Canadian UNICEF Committee
Canada Square
2200 Yonge Street, Suite 1100
Toronto, ON M4S 2C6
Canada
www.unicef.ca

Irish National Committee for UNICEF
25–26 Great Strand Street
Dublin 1
Ireland
www.unicef.ie

New Zealand Committee for UNICEF
Level 5
11 Aurora Terrace
Lambton
Wellington, New Zealand
www.unicef.org.nz

United Kingdom Committee for UNICEF
Africa House
64–78 Kingsway
London WC2B 6NB
www.unicef.org.uk

United States Fund for UNICEF
333 East 38th Street GC–6
New York, New York 10016
U.S.A.
www.unicefusa.org

To find e-mail addresses for UNICEF's country and regional offices:
www.unicef.org or
addresses@unicef.org

Other child-related websites:

Child Rights Information Network
www.crin.org

International Save the Children Alliance (ISCA)
www.savethechildren.net

Oxfam International
www.oxfaminternational.org